Alfred's Premier Piano Express

Dennis Alexander, Gayle Kowalchyk, E. L. Lancaster, Victoria McArthur & Martha Mier

FOREWORD

Alfred's *Premier Piano Express Repertoire, Book 4* includes motivational music in a variety of styles, reinforcing concepts introduced in *Premier Piano Express, Book 4*. The pieces (including one duet) in this book correlate page by page with the materials in *Premier Piano Express*. They should be assigned according to the instructions in the upper-right corner of each page of the book.

All original music (including one duet) was composed or arranged by Dennis Alexander and Martha Mier. Selections of standard repertoire by D. Scarlatti, Rameau, Bartók, Schumann, Attwood, von Weber, Gurlitt, C. P. E. Bach, Schytte, Heller, and Benda also are included. The music in this book can be used as supplementary repertoire for any method. Students will enjoy performing these pieces for family and friends in a formal recital or on special occasions.

ONLINE ACCESS INCLUDED

Audio Performances and Orchestrated Accompaniments

TNT² Practice Software

To access the audio and software, visit:
alfred.com/redeem

Enter this code:
00-48633_228822

CONTENTS

ISBN-10: 1-4706-4343-X
ISBN-13: 978-1-4706-4343-0

Alfred Music
P.O. Box 10003
Van Nuys, CA 91410-0003
alfred.com

Cover Images:
Piano photo courtesy of Yamaha Corporation • Stack of paper image © Getty Images

Use with Premier Piano Express, Book 4, Review, pages 4–5.

A Cliff Hanger!

Dennis Alexander
Martha Mier

Use with Unit 1, pages 8–9.

Missouri River Ballad

Dennis Alexander
Martha Mier

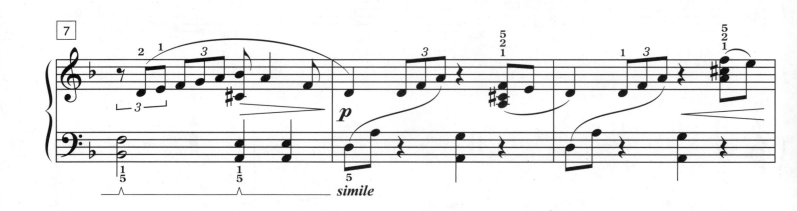

5

Use with Unit 2, pages 10–11.

Minuetto  2

(Second Movement from *Sonata in C Major*)

Domenico Scarlatti (1685–1757)
K. 73b: L. 217

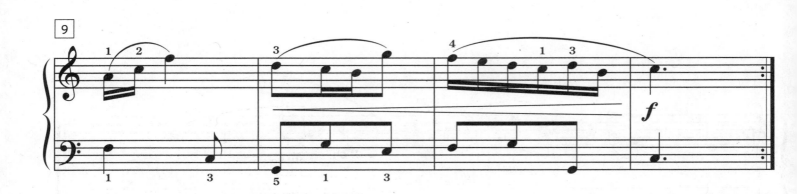

Use with Unit 2, pages 14–15.

Rondino 3

Jean-Philippe Rameau
(1683–1764)

A Little Softshoe 🔊 4

Dennis Alexander
Martha Mier

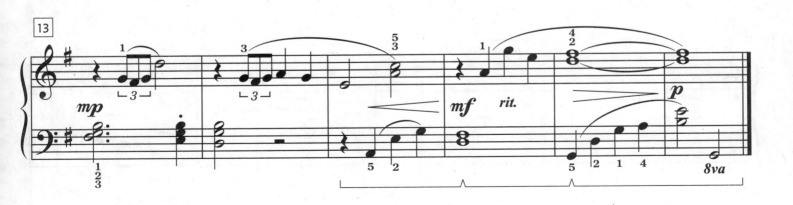

Hang Gliding

Use with Unit 3, pages 20–21.

Dennis Alexander
Martha Mier

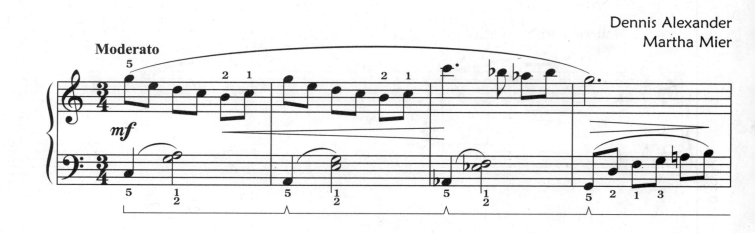

Use with Unit 4, page 26.

Teasing Song 5

Béla Bartók (1881–1945)
Sz. 42

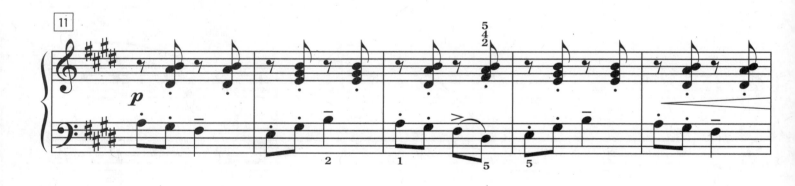

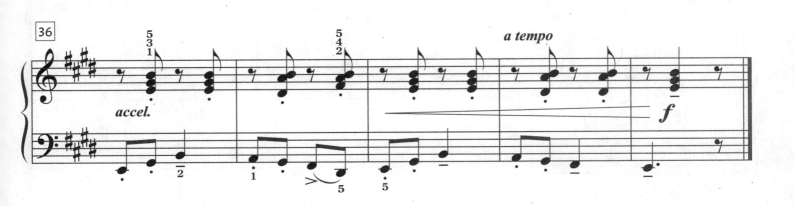

Use with Unit 5, pages 30–31.

Soldier's March 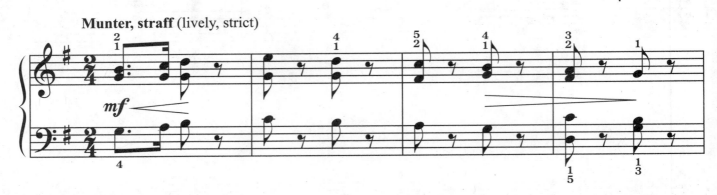 6
(from *Album for the Young*)

Robert Schumann (1810–1856)
Op. 68, No. 2

Use with Unit 6, page 33.

Sonatina in G Major 🔊7
(First Movement)

Thomas Attwood
(1765–1838)

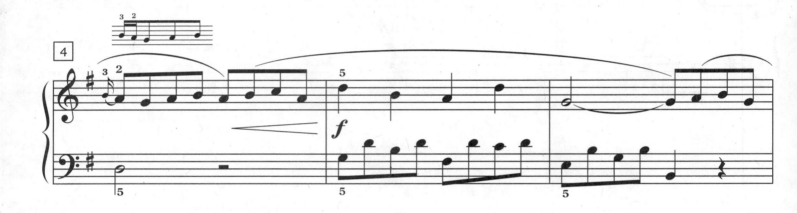

Use with Unit 6, pages 38–39.

Climbing the Pyrenees*  8

Dennis Alexander
Martha Mier

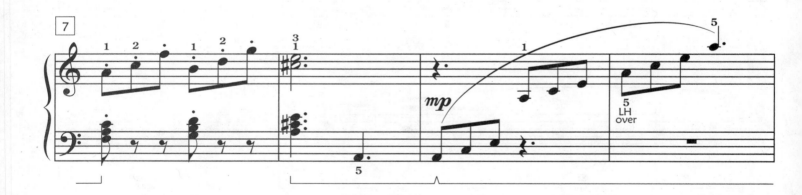

* The Pyrenees Mountains form the border between France and Spain.

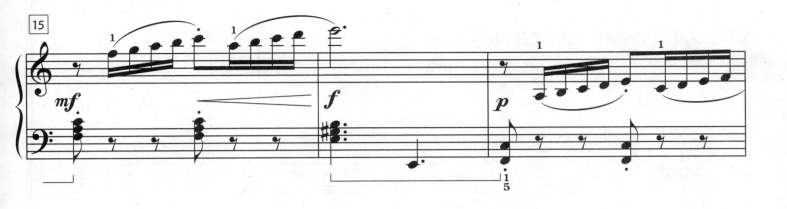

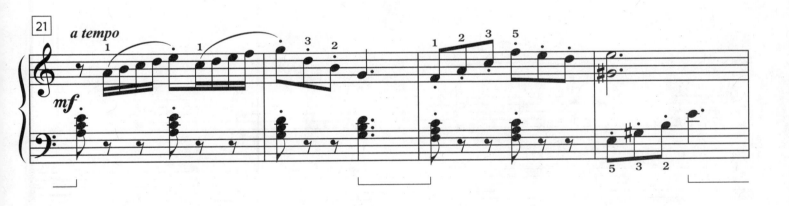

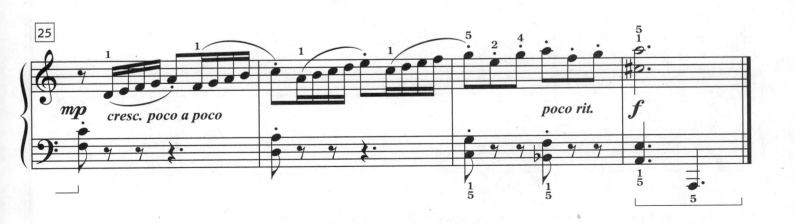

Use with Unit 7, pages 42–43.

Downtown Jazz

Dennis Alexander
Martha Mier

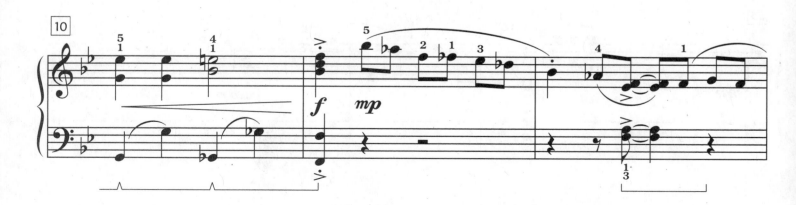

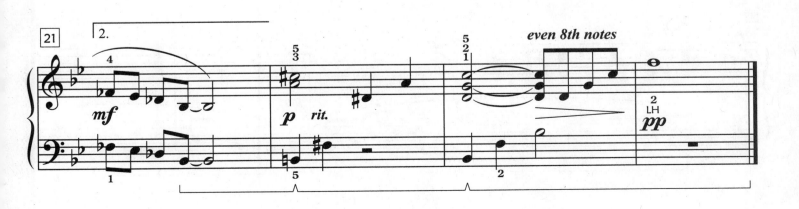

Use with Unit 7, pages 46–47.

A Note from the Heart

Dennis Alexander
Martha Mier

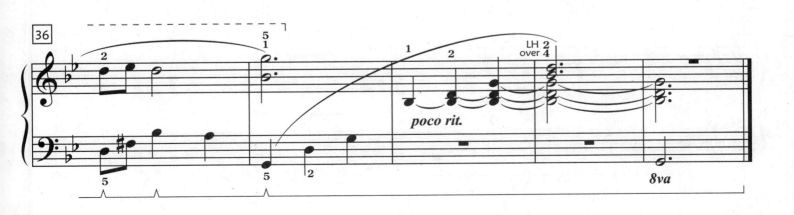

Use with Unit 8, pages 48–49.

Serenade de Seville* 🔊 10

Dennis Alexander
Martha Mier

* Seville is a city in southern Spain known for its art and literature.

Use with Unit 8, page 50.

Scherzo 🔊 11

Carl Maria von Weber
(1786–1826)

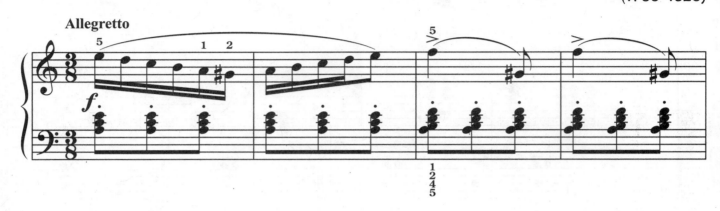

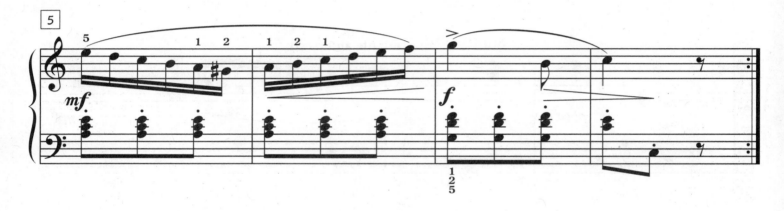

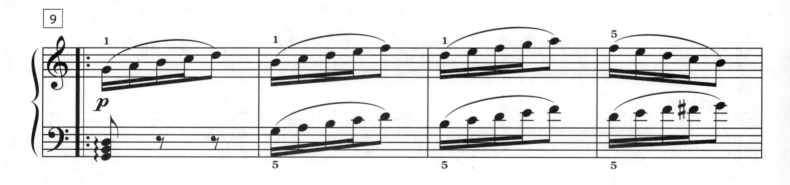

Use with Unit 9, pages 54–55.

Waltz in B Minor

Cornelius Gurlitt (1820–1901)
Op. 205, No. 10

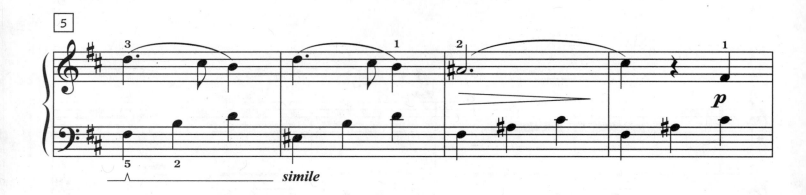

Use with Unit 10, page 61.

Solfeggio* in C Minor 🔊13

Carl Philipp Emanuel Bach
(1714–1788)

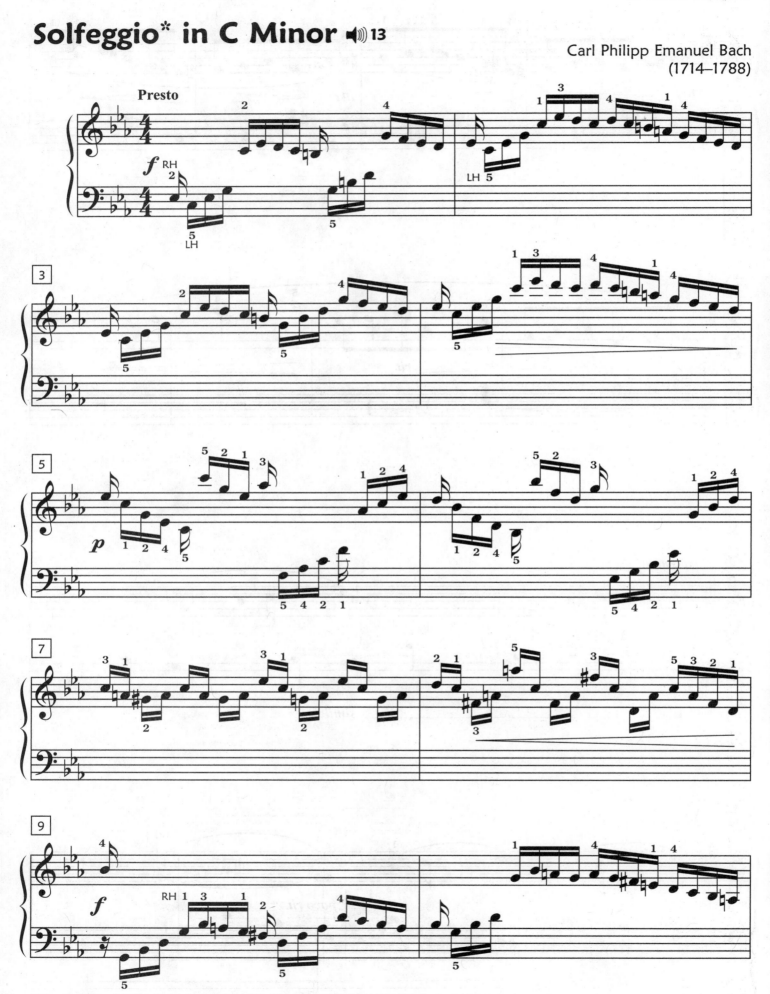

* A *solfeggio* is a vocal exercise sung with syllables (do, re, mi, etc.) for the notes.

Use with Unit 11, page 64.

Etude in D Major

Ludvig Schytte (1848–1909)
Op. 108, No. 7

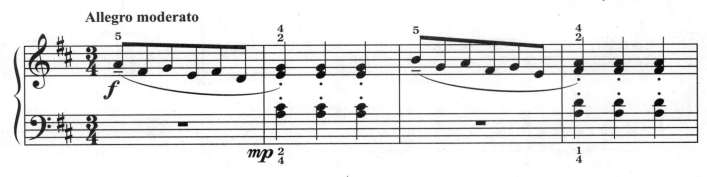

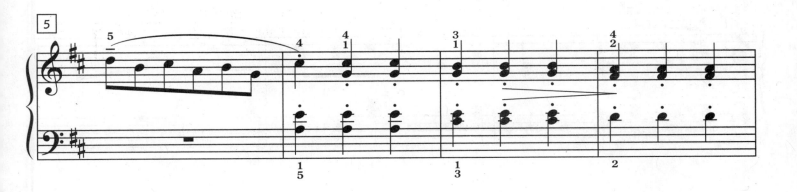

Use with Unit 11, pages 65–67.

The Wild Rider 14
(from *Album for the Young*)

Robert Schumann (1810–1856)
Op. 68, No. 8

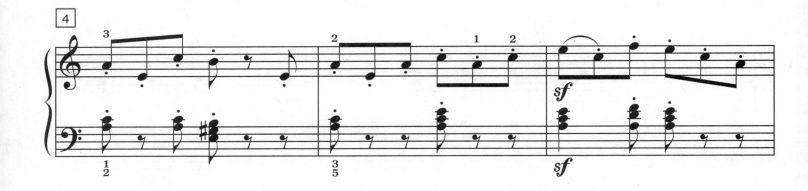

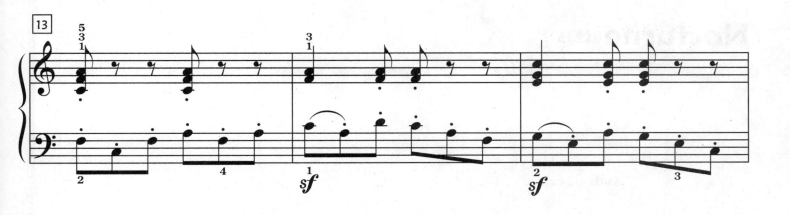

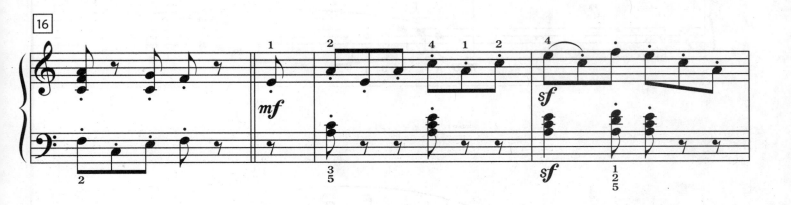

Use with Unit 12, page 75.

Nocturne 🔊 15

Dennis Alexander
Martha Mier

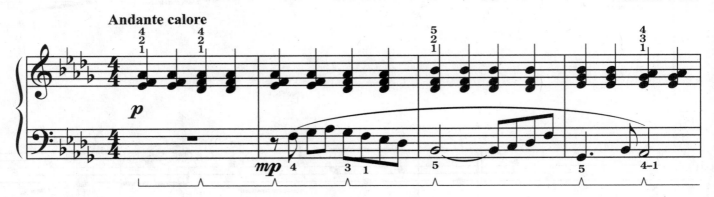

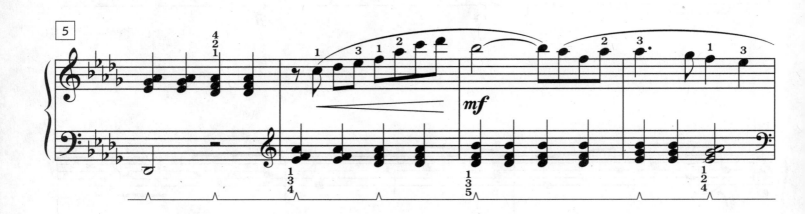

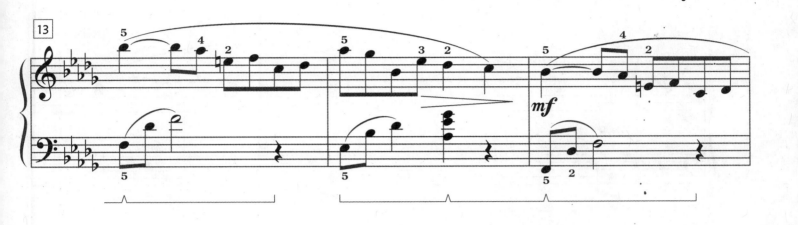

Use with Unit 13, page 76.

Emerald Rhapsody

Dennis Alexander
Martha Mier

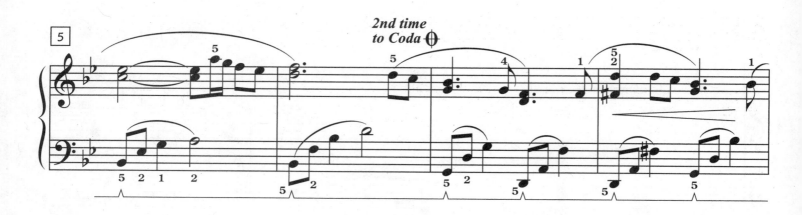

Use with Unit 13, page 78.

Jazz Reflections 🔊 16

Dennis Alexander
Martha Mier

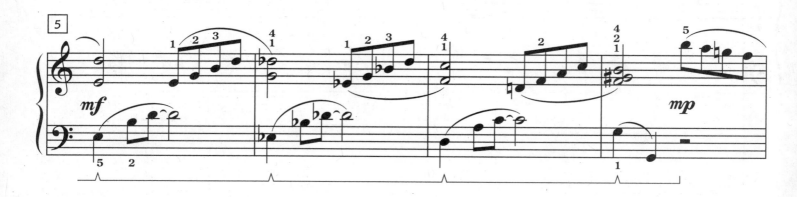

Use with Unit 14, pages 84–87.

The Avalanche  17

Stephen Heller (1813–1888)
Op. 45, No. 2

Use with Unit 14, pages 88–89.

Reverie 🔊 18

Dennis Alexander
Martha Mier

Use with Unit 14, pages 90–93.

Sonatina in A Minor 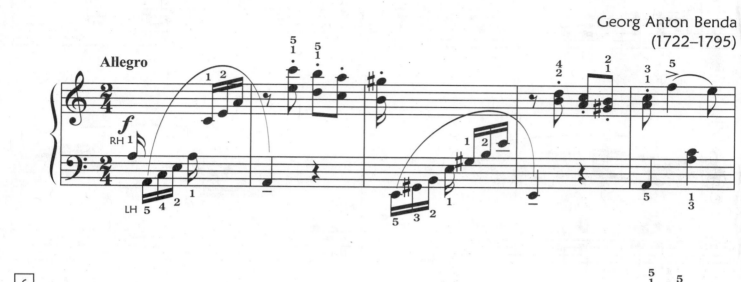 19

Georg Anton Benda
(1722–1795)

D. C. al Fine

Use with Unit 14, pages 94–95.

Magnolia Rag 🔊20

Dennis Alexander
Martha Mier

With a steady beat

Use with Unit 14, page 96.

Wildflower Rag

Secondo

Martha Mier

Wildflower Rag

Primo

Martha Mier

Secondo

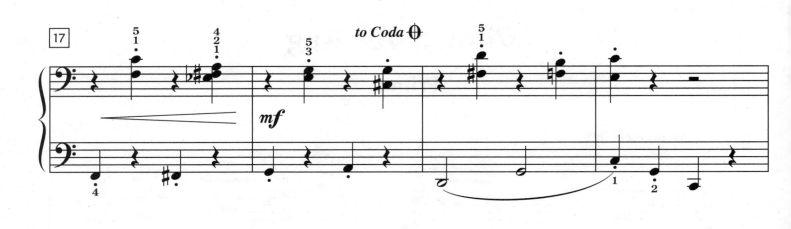

Primo

Audio Performances and Accompaniments

Stream or download audio performances on acoustic piano and orchestrated accompaniments for selected pieces in the book. Identified by a speaker icon (🔊) with a track number next to the title in the book, each selected piece includes two versions of audio:

- An acoustic piano performance at **performance tempo**.

- An acoustic piano performance at **practice tempo**.

Practice Software

For a more versatile practice experience, download the TNT 2 practice software, which allows the user to adjust the tempo of each track. Check the included Read-Me file for system requirements and installation instructions.